Stories About Jesus

Bible stories, activities, and a devotion

for Young Readers™

Illustrated by Jenifer Schneider

STANDARD
PUBLISHING
Cincinnati, Ohio

The Standard Publishing Company, Cincinnati, Ohio. A division of Standex International Corporation
© 1996 The Standard Publishing Company. All rights reserved. Designed by Coleen Davis
Printed in the United States of America. ISBN 0-7847-0542-9

Wild Winds and Waves Obey

from Matthew 8, Mark 4, and Luke 8

Jesus was tired.

All day long he had been teaching

from a boat on the lake.

When evening came,

Jesus said to his disciples,

"Let's go over to the other side

of the lake."

In the back of the boat,

Jesus went to sleep.

Then a wild storm began.

The wind howled, and waves

came over the sides of the boat.

"We are in danger!"

cried the disciples.

The disciples woke up Jesus.

"Teacher, Teacher, save us!"

they cried.

"Don't you care

that we are going to drown?"

Jesus got up.

He turned to the roaring waters.

"Quiet!" he said. "Be still!"

The wind went away.

The waves were still.

Jesus said to his disciples,

"Why are you so afraid?

Where is your faith?"

"What kind of man is this?"

the disciples asked each other.

"Even the wind

and the waves

obey him!"

Enough for Everyone

from Matthew 14, Mark 6, Luke 9, and John 6

Jesus and his disciples were busy.

"Take away my sickness,"

said a man.

"Heal my son," said a woman.

Jesus and his helpers did not rest.

"Get into this boat," said Jesus.
"We will go to a quiet place
on the other side of the lake."
The people ran around the lake
to meet Jesus there.
But Jesus was not angry.
"Bring the sick to me," he said.

Late in the afternoon,

Jesus' disciples said,

"Send the people to town

for food."

"No," said Jesus.

"We will feed them."

Andrew found a boy

with five loaves of bread

and two small fish.

"But that is not enough

to feed a crowd," said Andrew.

"Tell the people to sit

on the grass," said Jesus.

Jesus thanked God for the food.

He broke the bread and fish

into pieces.

"Give the food to all the people,"

Jesus told the disciples.

Five thousand men,

plus women and children,

had enough to eat.

The leftovers filled twelve baskets.

"Jesus must come from God,"

the people said.

Then Jesus quietly went up

the mountainside to pray.

Let the Children Come

from Matthew 19, Mark 10, and Luke 18

Some mothers and fathers

came to Jesus.

They carried babies in their arms.

They held their boys and girls

by the hand.

"We want Jesus

to pray for our children,"

the mothers and fathers said.

"We want Jesus

to give them his blessing."

But Jesus' disciples tried to stop

the mothers and the fathers.

"Get back!" they said.

"Can't you see that Jesus is busy?

He does not have time

for children!"

Jesus heard his disciples.

He reached out his arms
and called to the children.

"Let the children come to me,"
he said. "Don't stop them."

Jesus told his disciples,
"The kingdom of God
belongs to children like these!
Everyone needs
the simple faith of a child
to enter the kingdom."
Jesus hugged the boys and girls.
He held the babies.
And to the delight
of the mothers and fathers,
Jesus laid his hands
on all the children
and blessed them.

Big News for a Little Man

from Luke 19

Zaccheus the tax collector

felt squished.

He wanted to see Jesus.

But no one liked a tax collector.

No one would let

Zaccheus through

to the front of the line.

Then Zaccheus

had an idea.

He climbed a tree!

"Hello, Zaccheus,"

said a gentle voice.

Zaccheus looked down.

The voice belonged to Jesus!

"Come down quickly," said Jesus.

"I must stay at your house today."

"At *my* house?" said Zaccheus.

"Of course," said Jesus.

Zaccheus was happy.

He welcomed Jesus to his house.

People in the crowd were saying,

"Zaccheus is a bad man!

Jesus has gone to the house

of a liar and a thief!"

"What the people say is true,"
Zaccheus told Jesus.

"I have cheated people.

But I am sorry."

"I know," said Jesus.

"That is why I came."

Zaccheus decided

to make things right.

"I will share with the poor,"

he said.

"And I will pay back

everyone I cheated.

I will give back

extra money besides."

Jesus was pleased.

"This is a good-news day,"

he said.

Find the Way

Jesus' disciples are afraid of the storm. Help them get to the other end of the boat to wake up Jesus.

Connect the Dots

How did Zaccheus see over the crowd when Jesus came? Connect the dots to find out.

A Big God for Big Problems

Have you ever had

a big problem?

Do you have a friend

with a big problem?

Sometimes parents divorce.

A grandparent dies.

Your best friend moves away.

You have trouble

doing your schoolwork.

Jesus knows that children

can have big problems.

That is why he said,* "Let the

little children come to me."

He wants you to talk to him

about all your problems,

big *and* small.

Matthew 19:14

When there is trouble at home,

or when you are very sad,

Jesus cares.

If you are having problems

at school,

Jesus cares.

The Bible says,*

"Give all your worries to him,

because he cares for you."

Our God will help us

with every problem,

no matter how big!

*1 Peter 5:7

A Verse to Learn

☆ Give all your worries to him,
because he cares for you.
1 Peter 5:7

A Story to Read

☆ "Let the Children Come"
on page 346 of *The Young Reader's Bible,*
or
☆ Mark 10:13-16

Something to Pray

☆ God, I'm glad you care about me and my
problems, big or small. Please help me
with this problem: __________ .

Something to Do

☆ Make a prayer list. Print your problems on one
side. Leave space to write in God's answers.

There are many other *YoungReaders* products for you and your children to enjoy!

Look for these at your favorite Christian bookstore.

The Young Reader's Bible (24-03950). Kids 5 to 8 who are reading on their own will feel right at home with this age-appropriate Bible. From Genesis to Revelation, all 70 stories are short enough to finish in one sitting. It's the perfect way to start a child on a lifetime of personal Bible reading. Features include maps of Bible lands, time line, illustrated Bible who's who, "How Did We Get the Bible?" and a glossary.

The Young Reader's Bible on Cassette (24-23950). Capture all the fun and excitement of The Young Reader's Bible with this 110-minute cassette! Narrated by young children, all 70 stories from the original Young Reader's Bible are included with background music and sound effects that help capture a young child's imagination. Use the cassette as a great read-along companion to The Young Reader's Bible or as a stand-alone audio book. Great for traveling and bedtime, too!

Devotions for Young Readers (24-02756). One of the greatest things a child can learn is the importance of spending time alone with God. Now children will look forward to their own quiet time with Devotions for Young Readers. This collection of 52 devotions features the same artwork and easy-to-read format as the best-selling Young Reader's Bible. Each devotion contains a passage of Scripture, a corresponding Young Reader's Bible story, and activities that encourage children to put each lesson into action.

The Young Reader's Bible Double Fun Pads. These compact activity books are really two books in one—just flip them over to start a whole new set of fun activities. And after kids complete an activity, they can color in the page. A fun and challenging way to learn about the Bible. Great for traveling, too!

Double Fun Pad #1 (23-22107)
Double Fun Pad #2 (23-22108)